THE PATH TO RESILIENCE
Photo Book

Written by Jamie Lynn Tatera
Photographs by Jorie Johansen

Copyright © 2020 by Jamie Lynn Tatera

All rights reserved. No part of this book may be reproduced, stored in a retrieval system or transmitted by any means—electronic, mechanical, photocopy, recording, or otherwise—without the written consent of the author.

Published in the United States by Wholly Mindful, LLC.

Wholly Mindful is a trademark of Wholly Mindful, LLC. Milwaukee, WI.
Whollymindful.com

Library of Congress Cataloging-in-Publication data is available.
ISBN 978-1-952848-00-1 (PB)
ISBN 978-1-952848-01-8 (HC)
Ebook ISBN 978-1-952848-02-5

Printed in the United States of America

Book design by Jorie Johansen

For Everyone, including you.

What is the Path to Resilience?

The path to resilience is not about "trying harder" in the conventional sense of the word. Resilience involves moving with the flow of life rather than against it - navigating the currents so that we can steady ourselves, achieve our goals, and help others. On this path we give ourselves permission to be human—to be imperfect and have difficult emotions, and we also empower ourselves with skills to become the best version of ourselves.

An integral part of this path is the practice of A.N.D. (Allow, Nurture, and Discover™).

- "A" is for Allow. On the path to resilience we become aware of our thoughts, feelings and body sensations. Avoiding challenging emotions leads to stress and struggle. Noticing and allowing creates the space for a skillful response.
- "N" stands for Nurturing a healthy mind. Healthy mind skills include both cultivating compassion for our difficulties, and also growing mindfulness, gratitude, kindness and inner strengths.
- "D" is for Discover. Whereas resistance and fear narrow our perceptual focus, practicing curiosity paves the way for discovering new opportunities for greater freedom and happiness.

The path to resilience teaches simple, engaging and practical applications of research-based mindfulness, self-compassion, emotional intelligence and positive neuroplasticity. Through the integration of science, metaphor, story, and experiential practice, we learn to relate skillfully to difficult experiences and also intentionally create positive strategies for long-term resilience and well-being.

WHY MINDFULNESS?
A wild animal's brain is tethered to the present moment. Human beings need mindfulness because our minds have the amazing and sometimes problematic power to replay the past and imagine the future.

FEEL YOUR FEET

*We can wiggle our toes and notice the sensations of our feet.
Feeling our feet grounds our awareness in the present moment.*

WHAT YOU RESIST PERSISTS
When we try to make something go away, it tends to hang around. Noticing and allowing are first steps to dealing effectively with difficult thoughts and feelings.

NAME IT TO TAME IT
Naming an emotion, labeling a thought, or sharing an experience tends to make it easier to bear.

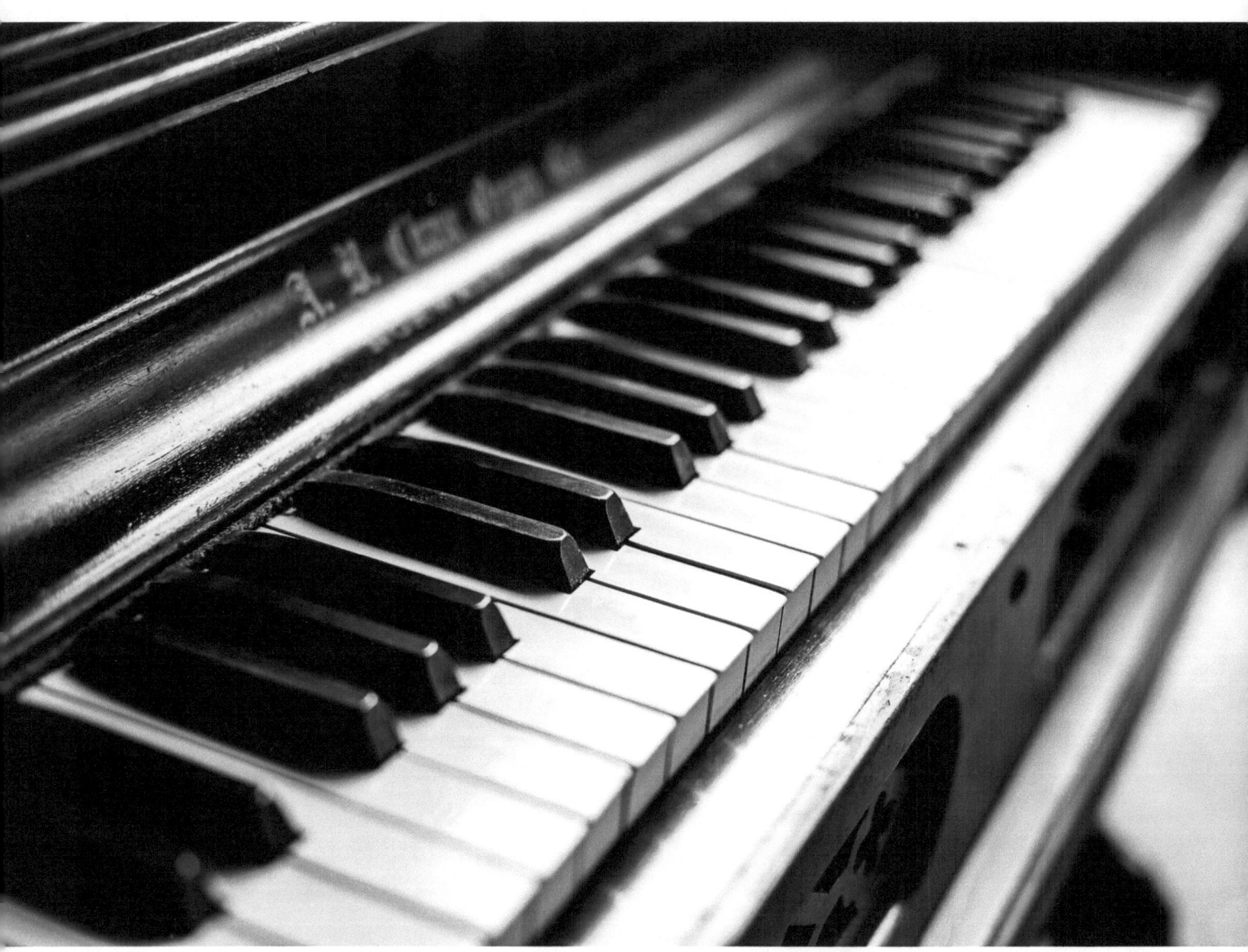

PIANO KEY FEELINGS
We need all of our feelings to be fully human. If we remove any "keys," we won't be able to play our beautiful music.

CONNECT AND THEN RESPOND SKILLFULLY

We can pause to connect with empathy and kindness before we problem solve.

BIG AND LITTLE FEELINGS
*We can notice and allow all of our feelings.
Little feelings count too.*

SHARE THE PLATE
When we experience an emotion, we can ask ourselves if other feelings are also present. Over time, we can share the plate with pleasant and unpleasant emotions. Kindness and curiosity can help us to share the plate.

CULTIVATE CURIOSITY
Curiosity facilitates growth and change.

HARD AND SOFT FEELINGS
Soft feelings like sadness or fear can hide under hard feelings like anger. Exploring soft feelings can reveal universal human needs that connect us to one another.

DISCOVERING GEMS

We can become curious about the needs and values that are at the heart of our emotions. Honoring these needs can lead to increased well-being.

FEEL IT TO HEAL IT

*Emotions have corresponding physical sensations in the body.
Feeling the physical sensations can help us to integrate our emotions.*

LISTENING TO SOUNDS
Mindful listening is noticing the sounds that arrive at our ears.

THE NEGATIVITY BIAS
Because the human brain evolved in the wild, our brains are programmed to constantly scan for danger and problems. We can intentionally rest our awareness on wellness to help ourselves experience well-being.

CONSTANCY OF CARE

Our bodies are nourished by the warmth of the sun, oxygen from the trees, and gravity that holds us to the earth.

THE INTERCONNECTEDNESS OF ALL THINGS

When we breathe in, the trees nourish our bodies with oxygen, and when we breathe out our carbon dioxide nourishes the trees. We are all interconnected.

SENDING KIND WISHES
Sending kind wishes to ourselves and others can help kindness to become a constant presence in our lives.

MINDFULNESS OF OUR SENSES

We can be mindful of any present moment experience. We can be mindful of thoughts, emotions, and each of our five senses.

WHAT IS THE WEATHER LIKE IN YOUR MIND?

The weather patterns in our mind are always changing, but our awareness is like the unchanging sky that holds the weather. Our equanimity grows as we are able to witness the weather passing through.

PUPPY DOG TRAINING

Our mind will naturally wander when we focus on a present moment experience. When our mind wanders, we can gently bring it back to the present again and again. Every time we return to the present moment is a celebration.

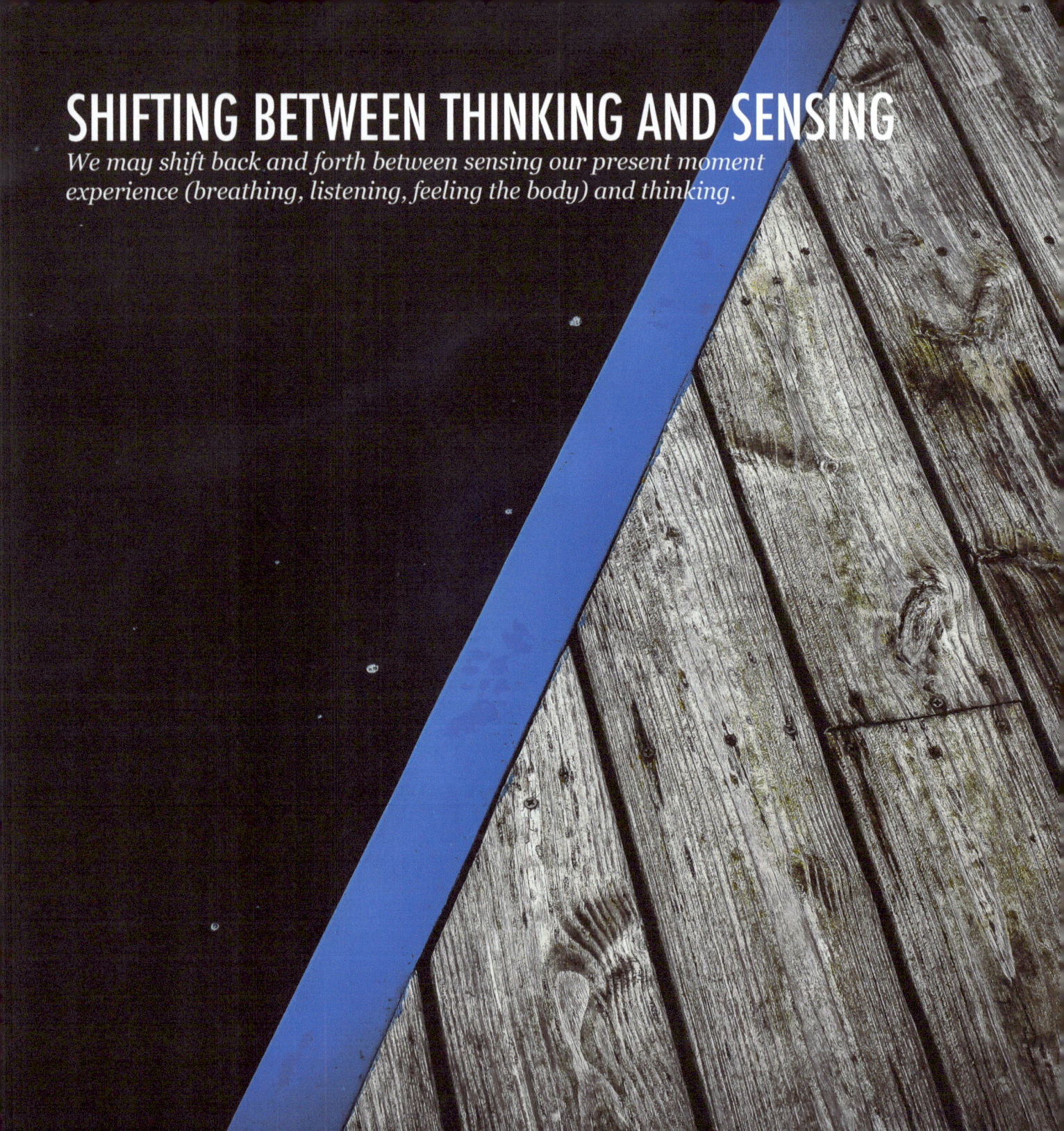

SHIFTING BETWEEN THINKING AND SENSING

We may shift back and forth between sensing our present moment experience (breathing, listening, feeling the body) and thinking.

THINKING AND SENSING SIMULTANEOUSLY

We may experience thinking in the background of awareness while we are sensing in the foreground of awareness, or vice versa.

GOOD LUCK, BAD LUCK - WHO KNOWS?

When we think that our present moment experience "shouldn't" be happening, we experience stress. Mindfulness is non-judgmental awareness of our present moment experience.

MINDFULNESS OF THE GARDEN OF THE MIND
We can observe the garden of our mind. We can apply wisdom to discern which thoughts lead to ongoing stress (weeds) and which thoughts lead to well-being (flowers).

UNDERSTANDING THE ROOTS

When we have a judgmental thought, we can ask these questions: "What values and needs is this thought trying to serve?" "How effectively does this thought honor my values and needs?"

A CHAIN OF THOUGHTS
A trigger (an event, thought, or image) can cause a cascade of thoughts and emotions. We might unconsciously link past experiences and stories to a trigger, which can create a chain of thoughts. We can become aware of the stories we tell ourselves.

SIDE-BY-SIDE THOUGHT CHAINS

When we have a stressful chain of thoughts, we can intentionally consider a more helpful story. Two thought chains can coexist side-by-side.

BROADEN THE PLATE
When we are focused on our thoughts, we can also notice our five senses. We can expand our awareness beyond thoughts to include more aspects of our present moment experience.

SELF-COMPASSION

Learning to pause and treat ourselves with kindness when we're having a difficult moment is the essence of self-compassion. We can also remember that we are not alone in our struggles.

COMPASSIONATE TOUCH
Offering ourselves a gentle touch when we are having a difficult moment is one way to practice self-compassion.

YOUR ARE A UNIQUE AND UNREPEATABLE CREATION!

It is both our quirks and our strengths that allow us to serve the world in an unrepeatable way. There will never again be another person on this planet with the same combination of weaknesses and gifts.

POSITIVE NEUROPLASTICITY TRAINING

Experiences change the structure of our brains. When we learn to notice and soak in the positive experiences in life, the structure of our brain changes in positive ways.

LIFE IS A SIDE-BY-SIDE EXPERIENCE
Our brains are designed for survival rather than happiness. If we don't intentionally notice the positive, we will automatically focus on the negative aspects of life.

SOAKING IN THE GOOD
When we bring our attention to a positive experience with all of our senses and stay with it for a few breaths, the experience becomes encoded into our neural structure.

PLANTING FLOWERS

We can grow well-being by purposely bringing our attention to positive experiences, practicing gratitude, and sharing in the joy of others' good fortune. We can grow flowers of well-being in the midst of difficult emotions.

NEGATIVE AND POSITIVE SIDE-BY-SIDE

We can complement complaining with an acknowledgment of blessings. Our goal is to see reality as it is - with its beauty and its thorns.

LITTLE THINGS COUNT TOO
Soaking in little positive things can fill our bucket over time.

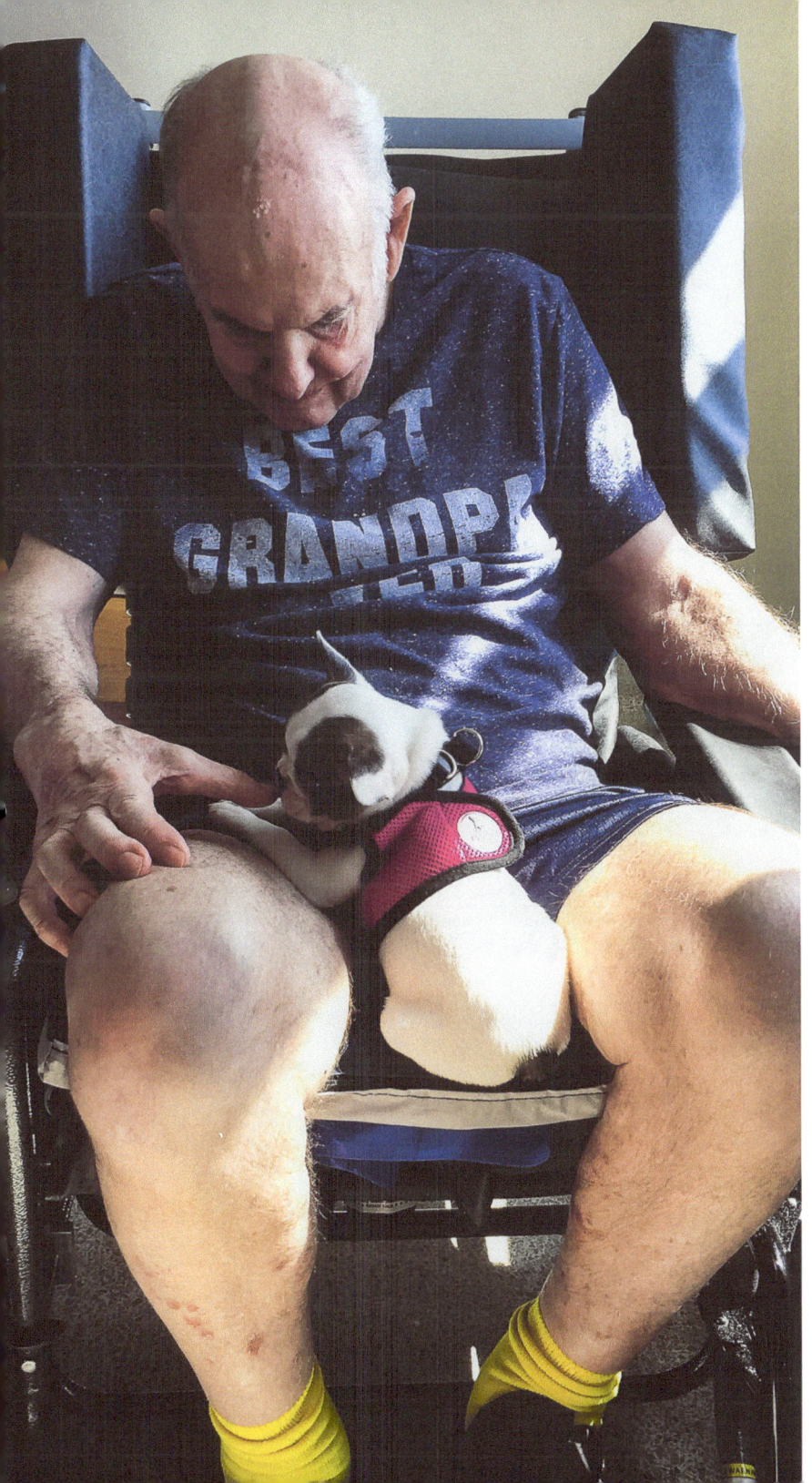

EXPANDING OUR CIRCLE OF WE

One way to grow well-being is to include more people in our circle of care. We can send kind wishes to grocery store clerks and people we might not otherwise think to include.

THE TWO WOLVES

We all have difficult emotions like anger and hatred as well as nourishing emotions like love and gratitude. We can meet the difficult wolf with compassion and grow the wolf of love.

LOOSENING THE KNOTS
We can send kind wishes to difficult people to loosen the knots of resentment. It is normal for side-by-side feelings to emerge when we send kind wishes to difficult people.

INTENTION AND PRACTICE
Which practices have you found most helpful? How can you support your intention to be well with these practices?

BUILDING A HEALTHY MIND

Skillfully tending to our thoughts and emotions needs to be complemented with caring for our bodies, nurturing healthy relationships, and creatively contributing to the world. Internal and external care work together to build a healthy mind.

Recommended Resources (authors who have inspired my own creative process and growth):
Bond, T. (2018). *The compassion book*. Orange Lake, NY: One Human Publishing.
Germer, C. & Neff, K. (2018). *The mindful self-compassion workbook*. New York: Guilford Press.
Hanson, R. (2018). *Resilient*. New York: Harmony Books.
Mindful Schools (https://www.mindfulschools.org/)
Siegel, D., & Bryson, T.P. (2012). *The whole-brain child*. New York: Bantam Books.

About the author:
Jamie Lynn Tatera is an educator, author, mother, and curriculum trainer. Her classes and curriculum creatively integrate the science and practices of mindfulness, self-compassion, emotional intelligence, and positive neuroplasticity. Jamie Lynn enjoys teaching learners of all ages: adults, teens, children, and elders. She offers private resiliency coaching to individuals and families, and she provides wellness and curriculum training for schools and organizations. Jamie Lynn's classes, blogs, and other resources are available at *www.whollymindful.com*. When Jamie Lynn is not teaching, she delights in hiking in nature, singing around campfires, and spending time with her friends and family in Shorewood, Wisconsin.

About the photographer:
Jorie Johansen's love for photography started as a young girl pouring over her parents' art and photography books. As the daughter of an artist and a teacher, she now gets to follow in the footsteps of both by working as a kindergarten aide as well as being the owner of a small family portrait photography business. She loves being in the outdoors, playing tennis, hiking, sailing and spending lots of time in her home away from home in Door County, Wisconsin. Jorie also loves to take (maybe too many) pictures of her wonderful husband, two active teenage sons and two dogs.

Special thanks to....

My mindfulness friends and colleagues Michaela Feriancikova Barrett, Anvita Mishra and Mary Novotny for their assistance and support in developing the Path to Resilience™ curriculum and photo book.

My mother, Gwen Tatera, for inspiring creativity in me, and my father, Jerry Tatera, for sharing his curiosity and wonder with me.

My two daughters, Maya and Anjali, for continually challenging me, inspiring me and believing in me.

My photographer, Jorie Johansen, for sharing her insight, beautiful photos and talent to help this book come to life.

Each of you. You allow me to share the jewels that I have discovered on this mindfulness journey with you.

Breathing in, I feel my body breathing in............ Breathing out, "Thank you."